RHYMES
FOR
OUR TIMES

by
Gordon Ross

William Sessions Limited
York, England

ISBN 1 85072 315 X

Printed in Helvetica Typeface
from Author's Disk
by Sessions of York
The Ebor Press
York, England

CONTENTS

VALUES

You may put a price on diamonds,
On property and shares,
You may envy other people,
For what isn't yours, but theirs,
But look inside those limousines,
They pay the price of fame,
They lose their precious privacy,
Which can't be found again.
Next time you feel 'hard done by',
They've more, when you have less,
Think, you may have what's priceless,
and that is, happiness.

PRICELESS

What would you rate most valuable,
In this world today?
The Kohinoor Diamond,
Some perhaps would say
For me, I am quite certain,
That most precious, in mans' life,
Is the love of a good woman,
Who's a faithful, caring wife.

IT'S THE GOSPEL

Dinner is now over, and you've stretched out your poor feet,
Started viewing East Enders, or Coronation Street.
Reached out for the chocolate mints, your world and all is well,
No, it's not the telly, It's your very own front door bell.
With great effort, you rise to your feet, the others haven't the will,
You say, "tell me later, what I've missed, and what she said to Bill"
You dash right down the hallway, and open the front door,
As soon as you see two of them, you know what they're there for.
Some are young, immaculate, look 'kitted out' that day,
Odds on they're American, at least they talk that way.
They want to put Joy into your life, but that's all very well,
But you were having all the joy you need, when they rang your bell.
Others are around middle age, unfashionable clothes,
Clutching little booklets, sport pink cheeks, brown hose;
Most of them are English, and do appear quite good,
They wish you to be also, if you think you could.
I've not mentioned their Religions, You'll know – of that, I'm sure,
But I certainly don't rebuke them, or close on them the door.
All trying, as they believe they should, to halt violence, hate, and greed,
And the world would be a better place, Should *all* realize that need.
I tell them I won't alter; I believe there's God as well,
But I put it to them simply, that as far as I can tell,
Out of numerous Religions, each 'fighting the good fight',
No-one can be that pompous, to think only they are right.
All, have a case to answer; *any* cause for good, I'm for,
Except those fought with violence, these I do abhor.
To those who strive for peace and good, give encouragement and hope,
By all means, give them your views, they definitely need more scope.
They're only human beings, trying in their way,
To make our world's tomorrow, into a happier today.

"What did she say to Bill", I asked, "did he go back home?"
" How the heck do I know, I was answering the 'phone!"

THEN AND NOW

Rambling over common land,
Made 'teenage', happy days,
The sweet smell of the heather,
Sighting Herons, Curlews, Jays.
Endless joy, with hosts of birds,
Around the trees and lakes,
Sharing, luscious habitat,
With Butterflies, Frogs, and Snakes.
Multitudes of wild flowers,
Pond life, Rabbits, Hares,
Squirrels, Stoats and Weasels,
Foxes, Badgers, in their lairs,
At first light,the Dawn Chorus,
Unequalled, Heaven sent,
The Songthrush, and the Skylark,
Gave 'their all', before they went.

Returning some years later,
To recapture joys of youth,
The Common Land was Out of Bounds,
I'm afraid that is the truth,
Our land, contained by fences,
Some, ploughed up, flat, and spoiled
The Death of Conservation,
For which generations, toiled.
Very little of the natural woods,
No wild life, oh so rare,
Nettles, Hemlock, and Dandelion,
Were bowed, in mourning, there.
How we've failed our children,
With lack of future vision,
Banned from Nature's habitats –
Condemned, to television.

WORRY

Why do people worry?
It doesn't help them cope,
It maximizes tension,
And minimizes hope.
Should worrying *be* the answer,
Then *do*, with all your might,
But never, in a million years,
Will worry put things right.
Sometime, in the future,
You *will* look back, and see,
That time alone, solves problems,
And much wiser you will be.

REALITY

Fashion models in a Magazine,
The 'Star' in a big movie,
With makeup, hairdos, lavish clothes,
All look rather 'groovy'.

But compare them with the natural girl,
Pure, and fair of skin,
Who doesn't have to force a smile,
Whose beauty is within.

Let magicians create illusions,
But they are not for me,
The purity of honesty,
Is all I need to see.

THE THIRTIES

Boots and shoes cost far too much,
I went to school in clogs,
No wash machines; 'dolly sticks' and tubs,
Were used to clean our togs.
No carpets – lino only,
Covered solid floors,
And ice cold winds found every gap,
Through window frames and doors.
In winter, ice, thickly covered windows,
Even right inside,
No central heating – double glazing,
Thus, many people died,
No vacuum cleaners, or such like,
No stereos, TVs then,
Gas mantles, dim, our only light,
Wrote with bottled ink and pen.
In ovens, in the fireplace,
Mum used to bake our bread,
Log fire, our flat irons heated,
She 'ironed' – we slept in bed.
Cars were then a rarity,
'Two stroke' motor bikes, came our way,
Distinctive sound – their approach,
Was heard a mile away.
Dad walked many miles to work,
Long hours of toil and strain,
Later, a 'push bike' he acquired,
This helped to ease his pain.

We took our 'holiday', once a year,
A day at the seaside,
Arranged through the local Sunday School,
Ice creams and donkey rides!
Some school holidays we 'picked potatoes',
At farms spread far apart,
Filled our buckets, to the top,
Took them to waiting carts.
We weren't paid very much, I know,
But soon the pennies mounted,
And in very hardest, of hard times,
Every penny counted.
To the Doctor we paid a shilling a week,
He was pleasant, patient and kind,
No one better on this earth,
Could you hope to find.
To everyone he was a friend,
In which they could confide,
And always kept a jar of sweets,
To soothe a crying child.
Away for a day, house could be left,
without locking - that's a fact,
You knew full well, when you returned,
Everything would be intact.
Despite poverty in 'the Thirties',
There was more honesty and trust,
Less selfishness, greed and envy,
Vandalism, crime and lust.

JACK'S ROBIN

Jack had a Reliant Robin,
It was his pride and joy,
A friend he could rely on,
Quick transport, and his toy.
When he got behind the wheel,
He could never get 'his fill',
Off like a racing driver,
Round the corners, up the hill.
From one to a hundred 'em pee aitch',
In just five seconds flat,
If you'd just had your dinner,
You soon got rid of that.
White knuckles gripping hand rail,
Eyes closed up real tight,
You suddenly became Religious,
And prayed with all your might.
Jack was into D.I.Y.,
He bought a piece of board,
Secured it to his roof rack,
Into the sky he soared.
It really was quite scary,
He barely missed a tree,
And landed in the garden,
Of number ninety three.
Out came a charming lady,
Of Jack, she took a shine,
And said to him, quite sweetly,
"Drop in again sometime".
Big Dipper, Helter Skelter,
Theres something they all lack,
As there's nothing beats a Robin,
Piloted by Jack.

GREEN PEACE

If everyone was coloured green,
With no religious traits,
Desirous of just happiness,
Devoid of human hates,
How different life would be right now,
With all the world's great wealth,
The means to prevent famine,
Poverty, and ill health.

Of course, we could imagine,
We were *green* indeed,
Resolve Religious differences,
The world's now greatest need,
Really, we do all want the same,
Peace, ending all life's fears,
For each and every child that's born,
Lives of laughter without tears.

I remember well, my uncle Jack,
Who spread just happiness and mirth,
Saying "Lad, we make our own Hell,
Or Heaven, on this Earth".
I was very young, at that time,
Now I'm ancient, that is true,
But I'll remember it forever,
And I hope that you do too.

THE SENIOR, SENIOR CITIZEN

However much attention,
And care you may receive,
You still may feel neglected,
When carers take their leave.
But carers, friends and relatives,
Have many a cross to bear,
And you don't see their daily deeds,
And problems, that they share.
But most of all, when day is done,
Before they go to sleep,
They pray to God to keep you safe,
And Blessings on you heap.

GOODY GOODY

"Mum, I'll be good for fifty P,
Or chocolate, if you'd rather";
"You'll be good for nothing,
And be just like your father".

REWARD

Both Politics and Religion,
Are very much the same,
They can alienate the masses,
And for Wars may be to blame.

Peace epitomises Heaven,
Food and Caring promotes Health,
Pure greed is our worst enemy,
Not provision made from wealth.

Laws are made to be obeyed,
Rules should not be bent,
The Villain is the one who *starts* the chain,
of any gross event.

Those who believe in 'after life',
Need never lose their nerve,
I'm sure that simply everyone,
Will get what they deserve.

MISS BLAYDON'S CAKE

It was the kind of Christmas Day
You see on Christmas cards,
Snow, in abundance, everywhere,
Blocking the back yards.
Two Robins played upon the fence,
How bright their breasts did shine,
Children, with their sledges,
Up the hill, did climb.
The old lady, just opposite,
Opened her front door,
She beckoned me, "come over",
I went to see what for.
She was well in her eighties,
With greying ginger hair,
Fairly small, and quiet,
Darkest clothes, did wear.
She asked me to get mother,
Then begged her, time to take,
To go with Dad and us three kids,
To have some Christmas Cake.
As she was rather lonely,
And her friends were few,
We said we'd go on over,
"Somewhere around two".
So we did, as promised,
And sat down at the table,
She poured us all a sherry,
Of a well known label.
A big smile then, came on her face,
Rarely seen before,
She then produced, a big round tin,
From the sideboard, near the door.
She said she'd made a special cake,
And was so pleased we'd come,
She couldn't wait for us to eat,
And we would soon have some.
Majestically she took the tin,
Gently easing up the lid
Our eyes 'popped out' at what we saw,
– at least we thought we did,
The cake was wrapped in cotton cloth,

"Here we are", she calls,
With horror we all realized,
It was covered with Moth Balls.
She told us how she had kept it safe,
Protected for this day,
The smell by now, was choking us,
Wished we were miles away.
Hypnotized, we watched the balls,
Removed, one by one,
Placed carefully, in a bag,
Until the last was gone.
I admit the cake looked beautiful,
I'd never seen much better,
The recipe, she must have followed,
To the very letter.
She gave each of us, a giant slice,
Of Camphor laden treat,
My mind was in a turmoil,
As I shuffled in my seat.
Suddenly, by instinct,
A telepathic ruse,
We each had to distract her,
Whilst the others, cake could lose.
I brought a piece toward my mouth,
Tears streaming down my face,
As others filled their pockets,
Or any vacant space!
I emitted, one enormous sneeze,
My cake fell on the floor,
Her dog immediately gulped it down,
Left, howling, through the door.
Meanwhile, the old lady,
When empty plates she saw,
Said; "You must have liked it",
"You shall have some more!
We said it was delicious,
Perhaps later, we would see,
She hastily wrapped some up for us,
Saying, "Take this home for tea".
We wished her "Happy Christmas",
And then went on our way,
We've never seen the dog again,
To this very day!

OUT OF THIS WORLD

It was a peaceful bright and sunny day,
Birds sang in the trees,
The scent of late spring flowers,
Lingered on the breeze.
I strolled leisurely, through the park
On the pathway to the copse,
The squirrels scurried playfully,
Life suddenly felt 'the tops'
My heart then stopped a second,
Just steeped in awe, I guess,
At the vision I saw before me,
In a pale blue, silken dress.
Mesmerised by her beauty,
As, smiling, she stood there,
I just could not believe it,
Such perfection is so rare.
Detached from all reality,
She gently took my hand,
And we wandered without speaking,
To a glade with paths of sand.
She turned her face toward me,
Took the ribbon from her hair,
Which fell down, past her shoulders,
It was shiny soft and fair.

Her lips were silky, soft and moist
Like honey touched with wine,
I knew at once that I was hers,
She knew that she was mine
There was no frenzied passion,
Just tenderness and love,
True moments of sheer ecstasy,
One could never rise above.
I awoke quite suddenly,
A storm still overhead,
It had been there just earlier,
When I'd gone to bed,
It only seemed like seconds,
How could that be a dream?
The rain continued pouring down
Thought, 'what did it all mean?'
I pulled myself together,
Thought, 'dreams so good are rare
Gently brushing from my shoulder
One long, fair, silken hair.

BELIEFS

We all believe in something,
But we really aren't so clever,
Some weird ideas of 'wrongs' and 'rights',
Make no sense whatsoever.

It doesn't really matter at all,
Whether your 'City' or 'Suburban',
Or sporting a complete bald head,
A skull cap, or a turban.

You are simply a human being,
A challenge here to face,
To be good and to do good,
And make the world a better place.

Dispel all greed, hate, mistrust,
In friendships you must invest,
Be charitable and understanding,
Your God will do the rest.

LUCKY?

Don't envy people, who appear,
Much luckier than you,
Or all those bronzed and healthy,
Fall ill? they never do.
Who eternally, have the 'Golden Touch',
And just everything goes right,
No worries and no problems,
And sleep soundly through the night.
As, only after illness,
Can you recognize good health,
Only after poverty,
Does a little, seem like wealth.
And only stress and trauma,
Misery, pain, and strife,
Can make intervals of recession,
Look like Heaven, in your life.
It isn't being 'lucky',
That really brings you bliss,
It's the contrast between the two extremes,
Supposed, `lucky' people, miss.

LIFE

Pubs and Clubs do have their place,
With Darts or Pool, a friendly face,
The savoured drink, a little natter,
A well sung song, a Comedians patter.
But when I see a man alone,
I wonder if there's a wife at home,
With wailing child, and household tasks,
Desperate for help, but never asks.
Weary, tired, sapped of strength,
Needs to talk, and talk at length,
Misses bygone special hours,
A smile, the love, the bunch of flowers.
For some, 'too late', may be the cry,
But others still have time to try,
True love, in total, can't be measured,
And it should be, forever treasured.

TREASURE OR JUNK?

78s, 45s,cassettes and LPs,
Videos, and CDs, all waiting there to please.
We said when we retired, we would enjoy them all, together,
But there's no way we could do this, we'd have to live forever.
Greetings Cards of bygone years, are jamming all the drawers,
Loose snapshots and full Photo Albums, are in boxes on the floors,
There's pictures hanging over pictures, covering all the walls,
And everytime the door bangs, something accidently falls.
What used to be the spare room, is now filled to the top,
The house is like a minefield, when *is* it going to stop?
All spaces have been utilized, right down to the shed,
The door conceals an avalanche, which could just kill you dead.
To us every single item, holds memories which we share,
From the remnants of my old 'push-bike', and what's left of our first chair.
We make attempts, at intervals, to discuss what to throw out,
We stare at them for hours, then do a turnabout.
One day there'll be a clearance, but we won't be involved,
The house will hold our secrets, and all will be resolved.

BEREAVEMENT – A PROMISE

Sympathy, lessens not one's grief,
However much their wished relief,
By those who pray, with utmost hope,
That they find strength to help them cope.

No-one escapes the sad despair,
When one they love's no longer there,
But given time, as break of dawn,
The sun appears, and makes them warm.

Despite it's millions of miles away,
It gives us light and warmth each day,
As indeed, when brought to mind,
Will those we've loved, this you will find.

When in mind's eye, you see them smile,
You know your courage was worthwhile,
And each new day, your soul will flourish,
And all past memories, you will cherish.

As one who's had such pain as you,
I sincerely vouch, and swear it's true.

JIMMY

Jimmy was a 'grafter',
He worked from dawn till dusk,
And even on a Saturday night,
He would go out and busk.
Inevitably work took it's toll,
He ended up 'in dock',
A nervous wreck, afraid of life,
Loud noise, or ticking clock.
The 'way back' wasn't easy,
Two steps forward, one step back,
It took him many, many months,
To get life back on track.
This happened many years ago,
But he's kept a priceless treasure,
One stuffed blue two-toned Bambi,
Product of pain, not leisure.
He had to rest ten minutes,
After every single stitch,
Each hesitant manoeuvre,
To make, without a hitch.
The hell of concentration,
The trauma it imposes,
Beyond all normal train of thought,
Until life 'came up roses'.
There is a happy ending,
Jimmy's words can 'heal',
He listens to your problems,
And *does* know how you feel.

RESOLUTION

May, if today you cause one tears,
They be of joy to last for years,
Should today you raise a smile,
Your day has truly been worthwhile,
But, if today you cause one pain,
Resolve, you never will again.

LIFE'S TRUE ARTISTS

Pain, tension and depression,
exhilaration, hope,
Life's everyday experiences,
with which we have to cope.
Without words being spoken,
we all, our senses share,
Our joys, doubts and misgivings,
moments of despair.
Smiles for reassurance,
gentle squeezing for restraint,
Are all colours on life's canvas,
we share, and help to paint.
No human beings can do more,
than try to do their share,
And you will be forever blessed,
all those of you who care.

BINGO!

If it is to happen,
I'm sure tonight's the night,
I feel intensely lucky,
Everything's just right.
Overdue fulfilment,
The climax of my dreams,
The moment is approaching,
I'm bursting at the seams.

My pulses are now racing,
I'm ecstatically insane,
Yes! – nineteen, "Here!!" – it's Bingo,
Full House, Jackpot, Game.

MY BEST FRIEND

When 'Lady Luck' goes on vacation,
Then everything goes wrong,
The washing machine starts leaking,
Soon, the TV picture's gone.

The old car coughs and splutters,
Then, 'gives up the ghost',
The oven decides to go on strike,
Bang goes the Sunday roast.

The Electric kettle, 'in it's element',
Joins the happy throng,
The door bell goes on short time,
It 'dings', but doesn't 'dong'.

The central heating, suddenly goes "bang",
From the ceiling, water drips,
Can you retain your sanity?
With trauma, come to grips?

You can restrain your bottled anger,
You can make the chaos end,
For you have a priceless asset,
You call merely, 'MY BEST FRIEND'.

TO SOMEONE SPECIAL

I love you very deeply,
And if there was a way,
I'd shoulder all your burdens,
And take all your pain away.
Remember this forever,
You can, in me confide,
And I will be, as always,
There, close by your side.

CONTRAST

Sweating windows, pouring rain,
Water gurgling down the drain,
Heavy head, ruined plans,
'Bored to death', wringing hands.
The warming sun, the bright blue sky,
Song birds singing, way up high,
Carefree, happy, life's so good,
I savour joy; wish others could.

THE GOOD DOCTOR

Thank God for the good Doctor,
Who lets your bottom touch the chair,
Without checking for the third time,
That his wrist watch is still there.
One who listens to your symptoms,
Without stopping you in your tracks,
With a hasty diagnosis,
Without hearing all the facts.
There are very many people,
Who weather life's storms and gales,
Only go for consultation, when,
Too much illness tips the scales.
Yes, hearing patient's problems,
Is bound to take it's toll,
On weary, caring doctors,
Justly proud of their life's role.
A stitch in time saves nine, they say,
Good Doctors know the way,
That tomorrow's hours can be saved,
by minutes spent today.

VILLAGE SCHOOLDAYS 1940s

All things distasteful were “for your own good”,
“If you don’t eat your greens, you’ll get no pud”
How many times you were chilled to the bone,
Hearing, “You’ll get the belt when yer father gets home”.

When Dentist’s caravan appears in school yard,
Faces turned pale, like packets of lard,
The brave could play truant, “It’s only the cane”,
Odd ones stayed off with vague tummy pains.

The ‘Nit Nurse’ arrives, of elephant size,
A smile you don’t trust, evil glint in her eyes,
Vigorously mauls you like a great mountain bear,
Takes the greatest pleasure in tugging your hair.

I well remember one horrible day,
It was ‘Doctor’s and Nurses’, but no games to play,
Scarlet fever, Measles, Diphtheria jabs,
With needles like stair rods, and cotton wool swabs.

Sweets were ‘on ration’ and went very quick,
You would try anything you could chew, suck or lick,
Liquorice roots, Rennies, Honey Toffee – like glue,
Horlicks tablets, Oxo cubes, to name but a few.

One day, a lad, generous to the core,
Gave us some chocolate, and we went for some more,
It came from a shop, just down the street,
And without coupons, it was a great treat.

The meaning of laxative, our minds never crossed,
It was really good chocolate, and at little cost,
But the Battle of Britain began ten to four.
With a cavalry charge, to the one toilet door.

Just a brief glance, as wonder you may,
What was so different then, from today.

WRINKLES

I see only joy in wrinkles,
The stories they could tell,
Of problems met, and overcome,
And struggles to get well.

Absorbing pain of others,
Comforting the bereaved,
Relieving stress with kindness,
Not just in words, but deeds.

There's wrinkles from the laughter,
Induced, and gladly shared,
With those who'd missed it's presence,
As no-one ever cared.

Yes, wrinkles I'd be proud of,
If knowing, in the end,
That everyone in the whole wide world,
Was everybody's friend.

QUARRELS

Quarrels are as inevitable,
As clouds which hide the sun,
Although clouds don't last forever,
For soon, there's warmth and fun.

And clouds which you yourself create,
However large or small,
Can disappear, with two small words,
"I'm Sorry", that is all.

Proving who is right or wrong,
Is really no 'big deal',
It's pointless being unhappy,
When those simple words can heal.

Don't add to all those millions,
Who live their lives in sorrow,
For believing unsaid words today,
Could still be said tomorrow.

PRIORITIES

The endless lines of tortured souls,
The merciless baking sun,
Flies swarming, on sore aching eyes,
The prayers, for rain to come.
The scattered empty rice bowls,
That echo the despair,
Then, later, eerie silence,
For life that once was there.
The rich and famous congregate,
At the Charity Ball,
Food and drink, and laughter,
Fun and games for all,
The end result, brings only good,
The means, for cash, to raise,
But, how many lives, *could* have been saved,
In those preceding days?

Every second counts......yet the Band plays on!

WORDS

With dictionaries so full of words,
The brain can hardly cope,
But I believe the most prolific,
Are Faith, Peace, Love, and Hope.

SEPTEMBER THE ELEVENTH 2001

SEPTEMBER IN OUR LIFETIME
CANNOT BE THE SAME AGAIN,
THE BEAUTY OF THE FOREST TREES,
THEIR LEAVES, AS DOWN THEY CAME;
MINGLED WITH OUR THOUGHTS, FOR LOSS OF THOSE,
WHO SHARED WITH US OUR DREAMS,
WHICH BROUGHT OUR WINTER FORWARD,
AND EVERYTHING IT MEANS.
BUT SPRING – HOWEVER LATE IT COMES,
THROUGHOUT ETERNITY,
DOES ARRIVE FOR EVERYONE,
WHEREVER THEY MAY BE.